**TA**

INTRODUCTION
MY STORY

I. UNARMED SOLDIERS
II. THE ENEMY
III. THE ARMOR
IV. WE CRY TO GOD
V. YOU HAVE JOINED FORCES WITH GOD
VI. BASIC COMBAT TRAINING
VII. YOU ARE A SOLDIER; FIGHT!
VIII. THE GREATEST LOVE STORY EVER TOLD

Dedicated to all of you who listened to me, who advised me, preached to me, taught me and prayed for me in Jesus' name.

God Bless You.

    I miss you John

# Introduction

The words in this book have been written to those of you who do not feel loved. Your stories are many, but the pain is the same. God wants you to feel loved. He wants you to know exactly how he loves you.

I offer my story to encourage you and witness to you of the power of God's love and of the devil's defeat in my life. I want you to develop a story that will stand as a witness to the same. "… for the accuser of our brethren is cast down, which accused them before our God day and night."
"And they overcame him by the blood of the Lamb, and by the word of their testimony;…" -***Revelation 12:10, 11***

Lastly, I want us Christians to become more aware of our role as soldiers in the army for the Lord. We should always remember we are in battle. Your wounds do not take you out of the fight. You should use them to help you fight harder.

I pray for the peace of God in your lives. Amen.

## My Story

I have always had a mild personality. I am usually quiet and some would say shy. I believe I am just cautious. I am watchful and studious of people. I am a good listener and not a big talker.

I prefer to write about things. It does not take much effort for me to write something. I have been that way since I was a little girl. Since I am somewhat shy, writing helps me to express myself thoroughly. Writing takes away the fear of stumbling on words and it allows you to give the words color and an artistic flow. When I write, I don't feel the panic that comes with the thought of not looking right, or not sounding right. Writing makes your thoughts sound as if they just flowed perfectly from your mind.

I really enjoy the beauty of nature. I like to see the trees and the flowers and the sky and the rivers and lakes. I think it is the most beautiful picture the eyes can behold. I enjoy growing flowers. Watching life come right up from the ground is amazing. Flowers are the perfect, natural, decoration for any occasion.

I like to think of myself as a lover and not a fighter. If there is any way I can avoid confrontation, that is the way I want to go. Confusion bothers me. Though I tend to be a humble person, I am also strong willed with great determination. I am very strong.

As years have gone on, I have come to know the Lord. He has held on to me and I have held on to him. He has been all I had many times. I have learned to love people, but trust God. "Blessed is the man that trusteth in the LORD, and whose hope the LORD is."-*Jeremiah 17:7*
I do not expect people to be what they are not able to be. "And Jesus said unto him, Why callest thou me good? there is none good but one, that is, God."-*Mark 10:18.*

I was born to a mother, who was only 13 years old. She of course could not care for me. She had to rely on an overwhelmed, undereducated mother for help with raising me. My father was not there to help her. He too was very young. He made some bad choices in his life and he was in prison most of my life.

My mother does not talk about her life much. The things I do know are things I have seen myself and some I learned by chance. I understand she never wants to talk about them either. I do understand that her life has been far, far from what is called a pretty picture. I believe that if she thought about it or talked about it, she would probably start screaming and not stop for a long time.

When I was a little girl, I was sexually abused by my mother's second husband. I was awakened one night by him molesting me, while I was in bed. I did not know what was happening, but I knew my private areas were being invaded. I was so frightened, that all I did was cry silently until it was over.

In the words of a six year old girl, I told my mother what happened to me. I remember living at my maternal grandmother's house shortly after that. I told my grandmother, but she said I was making it up. There was some reason I did not believe her excuse for dismissing me. I think I did not believe her, because of her relationship with my mother. I never felt my mother and grandmother had a healthy relationship. I believe that unhealthy relationship transferred to me.

After a short stay with my grandmother, we returned to live with my mother's husband. One day, soon after, I overheard a conversation that made me believe my mother would be put in jail. The reason was that she did not get me out of that abusive situation right away. I loved my mother dearly and I was so afraid she would go to jail. I did not say anything else about the abuse. I remember feeling as though my world went black, when I knew not my mommy, nor anyone else would save me from the monster. That was the most heart wrenching pain I have ever felt. At the age of six I felt like I was on my own. I was terrified every night.

I began to withdraw. Nothing was fun anymore. I fought in my mind to believe that what I knew inside me was right. No one told me what was right or what was wrong, but somehow I knew. I refused to conform to what everyone around me would have me believe. I started desperately trying to take care of myself. Whenever my mother and her husband would say anything to me, I automatically turned away from it in my mind. I thought everything they said or did towards me would be wrong. I was trying to keep my sanity with all my might.

I was psychologically abused daily. Everyday my mother's husband would talk to me about sex, after my mother left for work. He was depraved. I remember having a belt tied around my neck once. He did those things to try to make me have sex with him. He told me that people in other families were doing the same things. He said that everybody just kept things a secret.

I once had to promise to have sex if I wanted to have a birthday party. I was told that I could have the party, but right before people started to arrive, I was told that I had to have sex first. I did not want the party that badly.

Looking back, I can see how he systematically made my mother see me as a problem child. He would badger her everyday about something he said I did wrong. It was never true, but it bothered my already overwhelmed, mother. She began to look at me as her enemy. She finally turned to me one day and screamed, "Just do whatever he says!" I knew she was trying to tell him not to bother her anymore. She had already given her silent permission for the abuse. Now, she was giving her verbal permission. I hear now, how maddening that sounds, but it was just everyday life for me. When I think about my childhood, there are hardly any memories I want to keep.

I think God was with me then, and he made

me know that what happened was horribly wrong. That must be why I knew it when nobody else thought so. When I was about 13, I felt so unloved, abused and rejected; I decided that I could not trust anybody. I began to try to commit suicide, but God would not allow me to be successful.

I started running away to live with my grandmother, when I understood how to ride on the bus. I was very emotionally disturbed from the life I had been surviving, but it was peaceful at my grandmother's house anyway. I went to school, came home and did my homework. I did not have many friends, but just being able to go home and have peace meant the world to me.

I did not go to church much as a child, but I do have a good memory of once going with my mother. I remember sitting in the pew having this feeling of happiness that I had not felt before. People had smiles on their faces and they were smiling at me (I remember those faces until this very day).

They seemed to really like me. I remember thinking that, "This must be love." If I had ever felt loved before, I could not remember. The people had loving faces. I felt safe. I wanted to stay. I can recall saying to myself or maybe it was aloud, "I want to be like Jesus, I want to be like Jesus." I do not remember how old I was and I am sure I did not fully understand what I was saying. I knew that they kept talking about someone named Jesus and I was feeling like someone cared for me. The preacher made it sound like Jesus was the person who loved people the most, so I wanted to be like him.

I am sure God saved me when I said, "I want to be like Jesus.", but life was a nightmare and I could not awake from it. There was a time that I turned away from God, because I thought he did not care. I believe I was saved from those words I spoke as a child, because I remember feeling a cold, eerie feeling when I said, "I don't believe in God any more." It felt as though something left me and I was alone. I learned to close myself up emotionally, so I would not feel all the pain.

As a teenager, I looked for love in so many wrong places. I was not sure what love was, so I accepted whatever from whomever. I just needed love. When I was 19 years old, I met a man. He was 14 years older than I was, but I had no problem with that. He made me feel safe. We became good friends. He wanted to get married, but I refused. I had seen my mother married twice and it made me think that marriage was awful. We lived together and everything was fine. John was the kindest person I have ever met.

I gave birth to two healthy sons. I had both of my sons by the time I was 21 years old. One day, when my children were babies, someone knocked on my door with information about a parenting center. I went along with my children to that center for years after that. I believe God allowed me to know of the center and gave me a desire to go there. I believe this, because I never would have imagined a place like it on my own. I thought that surviving was the best thing I could do. There was help there for me and for my sons There were social workers and others there to give assistance to parents. I was able to gain information about parenting that was useful. I received advice and encouragement, when I needed it. It was a place for the children to play and I was able to release some everyday pressure. That center was a blessing to me and my boys. I believe God directed me to that place for that purpose.

I became good friends with one of the ladies, who worked at the center. She is a Christian. We continue to be friends until this very day. Through 24 years now, she has encouraged me and advised me. I look to her for Godly wisdom. I thank God for her. I believe God placed her in my life, because I never thought to look for someone like her. She provided me with Godly wisdom and friendship, when I did not know to look for it. I have always seen her holding on to God, no matter her situation. This has strengthened my faith. I believe

God allowed us to meet for that purpose.

When my children were young boys, about seven and nine years old, I knew I had to teach them about the Lord. I began to go with my children to church regularly. God started revealing things to me and helping me to know that he did care, but evil is in the world. I realized that I had to fight through the pain. I found that God's word is alive. Those words begin to come alive in me as I study, and I accept them into my heart and ask God to help me live each one. "Even so faith, if it hath not works, is dead, being alone." -*James 2:17*

I thank God for the true Saints all over the world. The pastor at the church that I attended, with my children, helped me to begin the healing process from the abuse. I believed he knew God. He told a testimony of his life, which strengthened my faith. He told of how some men had tried to kill him, but he did not harbor hate in his heart. He consistently preached and taught God's word without compromise. There was a joy in him that could not be denied. He had love and compassion for people. His joy made my cold heart want to believe again. I began to hang on every word he spoke, because I wanted to know what he knew. I believe God sent him into my life for that purpose.

John died in 1999 when my children were both teenagers. That was a very rough period. John had been taking care of the children and me. He had soothed me after my nightmares. I know now, that I had a lot of emotions I had not expressed from the abuse I suffered. I probably had nightmares, because of those unexpressed emotions. John comforted me and made me feel special. His tenderness took away some of the bad feelings I had of myself. I will always miss him.

I have longed for a parent with wisdom and understanding to talk to, who could comfort me. I have never had my dad in my life, because he had been in prison. My dad was serving a natural life sentence in Louisiana, for heroin distribution, with no possibility for release. In 2006, because of a change in the law, my father was released after serving 30 years.

While incarcerated, he attended the New Orleans Baptist Theological Seminary Extension Center at Angola prison. In 1995, the New Orleans Baptist Theological Seminary established an extension center on the compound of Angola. Professors from the New Orleans branch instructed the classes. My dad was among the first of 30 enrollees. In May 2000, after four and a half years, he graduated with an Associate Degree in Pastoral Ministry and a Bachelor's Degree in General studies. He graduated along with the regular graduating class of 2000. He is living for the Lord. I now, have a father with the wisdom of the Lord to turn to when I need guidance.

I have been wounded on the battlefield. The enemy has tried to destroy me. That is what
an enemy does during battle. I actually feel

like the devil had been holding my head, trying to push it under water. God would not let me drown. He would always hold my hand and pull me up long enough to get a good breath.

When I was overwhelmed with pain, I felt all alone many times. I know now that I never have been by myself, and I give God all the glory and all the honor and praise for how he has kept me. Thank You Lord!

God has allowed me to know who he created me to be, though others would have me think I was not all God said I was. I believe God spoke to me once, calling me a winner. I was alone in a room. There were no other noises. I heard a sound that seemed to come from the bottom of my belly. It said, "You are a winner!" I have believed that since that day. I think the devil must realize that he should have killed me, to keep me from God's plan for my life. It's too late now!

I have made many mistakes and bad choices,

but God has continued to strengthen me through it all. He has revealed things to me, which helped me tremendously. I have had therapy to resolve past issues. I have learned that the journey with God is not going to be easy, but it will always be victorious. I am with the winner!

Now that I have battled many difficult times with the Lord on my side, I am able to talk to you about being a good soldier. If you are a child of God, never think your suffering is in vain. ***Romans 8:28*** says, "And we know that all things work together for good to them that love God to them who are the called according to his purpose." A soldier knows how to suffer, overcome, and go on to continue the fight.

Finally, I realize that it does not matter my situation, my psychological state or my emotional difficulties. I am a soldier that must always be prepared for battle. The enemy is always attacking whether I am strong or I am weak.

**Ephesians 6:10-18**

10Finally, my brethren, be strong in the Lord, and in the
power of his might.

11Put on the whole armour of God, that ye may be able to stand against the wiles of the devil.

12For we wrestle not against flesh and blood, but against principalities, against powers, against the rulers of the darkness of this world, against spiritual wickedness in high places.

13Wherefore take unto you the whole armour of God, that ye may be able to withstand in the evil day, and having done all, to stand.

14Stand therefore, having your loins girt about with truth, and having on the breastplate of righteousness;

15And your feet shod with the preparation of the gospel of peace;

16Above all, taking the shield of faith, wherewith ye shall be able to quench all the fiery darts of the wicked.

17And take the helmet of salvation, and the sword of the Spirit, which is the word of

God:
18Praying always with all prayer and supplication in the Spirit, and watching thereunto with all perseverance and supplication for all saints;

## Unarmed Soldiers

Many Christians are like unarmed soldiers on the battlefield. *Ephesians 6* tells us to put on the full armor of God. This enables us to fight against the wickedness in high places.

We, as Christians, do not realize that we are constantly in battle. You may be a student in college and studying hard to make good grades, you may be a mother and housewife fulfilled with the joys your family brings you, you may even be a homeless person struggling to eat every day, or you may be the CEO of a large successful company. It does not matter what pleasures, struggles, or responsibilities fill your days. If you are here on earth and you have given your heart to Jesus, you are a soldier in battle for the Lord.

I had been seeing myself as a victim only. I discovered in *Ephesians 6* that I am also a soldier. I am afraid that many of us are living selfishly. We have our own problems and that is all we see. I believe much wickedness would be stopped, if Christians would become armed soldiers and not victims. "Be not overcome of evil, but overcome evil with good." *-Romans12:21* We would then, be prepared for battle. I know that I always have to be prepared to fight. There will always be battles to win, for myself and others, against evil.

A soldier can never afford to forget that he is in a battle. When we do not read the word, we forget. When we do not pray, we forget. When we do not exercise our faith, we forget. When we do not realize the power of our salvation, we forget.

*Ephesians 6:11* tells us to put on the whole armor of God so that we might be able to stand up against the deceptions of the devil. Many of us are unarmed soldiers perishing for lack of knowledge *-Hosea 4:6*, leaving our weapons untouched. *John 10:10* says, "The thief cometh not but for to steal, and to kill and to destroy:…" in our lives and all around us. Evil will come to you no matter who you are.

***Ephesians 6:13*** says that we must put on the full armor of God so that we are able to resist and stand our ground in the evil day. You cannot wait until the evil day comes and then prepare to fight. The enemy will not wait for you to prepare.

We spend a lot of time trying to do all the things we think are good and holy, but we do not spend a lot of time being a good soldier ready for battle. We must be alert to do those things pleasing to God. We also must remember that we are soldiers. Soldiers are always preparing for battle. Without the armor God provides through his boundless might, we can have no victory for ourselves or others.

## GOD LOVES YOU!

For God so loved the world, that he gave his only begotten Son, that whosoever believeth in him should not perish, but have everlasting life.-*John 3:16*

**The Enemy**

Our enemy, the devil never forgets he is in battle. "Be sober, be vigilant; because your adversary the devil, as a roaring lion, walketh about, seeking whom he may devour:"-*I Peter 5:8*, "… He was a murderer from the beginning, and abode not in the truth, because there is no truth in him. When he speaketh a lie, he speaketh of his own: for he is a liar, and the father of it."-*John 8:44*
No, he never forgets. He is always searching for someone to attack with lies and deception.

It is so important for us to know that our enemy is the devil and not people. We spend much time and effort harboring bad feelings against one another. The word clearly tells us who the enemy is. "For we wrestle not against flesh and blood, but against principalities, against powers, against the rulers of the darkness of this world, against spiritual wickedness in high places."-*Ephesians 6:12*

I understood this one day as I listened to a preacher on television. He quoted Ephesians 6:12 and I realized that I needed to stop hating the person who hurt me, but I needed to focus that energy against the devil and his evil plans. I suddenly realized that my feelings of anger were doing me no good being pointed towards people. I discovered that the people were only being used to carry out the evil. The devil is the real mastermind. I know I must forgive. Holding on to feelings of hate and anger only hurt my soul. It is like helping the thing that hurt you, to continue to cause pain. Now I turn my anger towards the devil and I look to God for love, peace and wisdom to handle any problem or crisis.

The enemy has no rules to follow. Anything goes. He knows his fate is eternal damnation. He never forgets he is in battle, because he has no other hope. He wants you to turn away from God and go with him to hell.

Would you have any compassion if you were in his shoes? Would you care about innocent children? Would you care about hurting people? Would you care about anything? Well, just know that the devil does not care about anything! Your pain and suffering get no pause from him.

**JESUS LOVES YOU!**

I am the good shepherd: the good shepherd giveth his life for the sheep.-*John 10:11*

# The Armor

***Ephesians 6*** tells us how we can be protected from head to toe in the armor that God gives us. What Commander would send his soldiers to battle without armor? Let us try to understand the value of this armor.

We are to wear the belt of truth: "And ye shall know the truth, and the truth shall make you free."-***John 8:32***
The truth enables us to fend off the many lies the world offers. If you do not stand on the true word of God, you might fall for anything. The truth is different from reality. Reality is what men have agreed to accept, which makes it real to them. The truth is what God says, whether you accept it or not. God does not need anyone to agree with him.

There is the breastplate of righteousness: "But of him are ye in Christ Jesus, who of God is made unto us wisdom, and righteousness, and sanctification, and redemption:"- *I Corinthians 1:30* We can stand tall and forceful with the knowledge that we are in right standing with God.

We possess the helmet of salvation: "In whom ye also trusted, after that ye heard the word of truth, the gospel of your salvation: in whom also after that ye believed, ye were sealed with that holy Spirit of promise."-*Ephesians 1:13* We have eternal life! This means we battle with no fear of death.

Take the shield of faith: "But without faith it is impossible to please him: for he that cometh to God must believe that he is, and that he is a rewarder of them that diligently seek him."-*Hebrews 11:6* We must have faith in who God is if we are to win in any battle against the devil. We know that our natural bodies are not able to fight the supernatural wickedness; we must have faith in God's power.

We can stand firmly with our feet shod with

the preparation of the gospel of peace.-*Ephesians 6:15*.  Jesus lived, died for our sins and was resurrected.  *Matthew, Mark, Luke* and *John* recorded the gospel, so that we may believe. This good news should keep your spirit stirred with excitement!

Our sword is the word of God. "For the word of God is quick, and powerful, and sharper than any twoedged sword, piercing even to the dividing asunder of soul and spirit, and of the joints and marrow, and is a discerner of the thoughts and intents of the heart." -*Hebrews 4:12* When the word is preached and taught it is working in men's hearts.   When we witness to others the word is working. We also see in *Matthew 4* how the devil tempted Jesus.   Jesus wielded the word at the devil's every temptation and the devil left him.   This shows perfectly what a powerful weapon we have in the word of God.

Overall, *Ephesians 6* tells us to pray. We must always pray for one another.   Let us remember to pray for all the saints everywhere. We must not pray only for our families, our communities, our nation and our leaders. Let us pray for other families, other communities, other nations and leaders in places all over the world. Soldiers should continuously be giving thanks to, making pleas to and taking commands from our general, the Lord our God. Our armor is mighty in the Lord!

## JESUS LOVES YOU!

Nevertheless I tell you the truth; It is expedient for you that I go away: for if I go not away, the Comforter will not come unto you; but if I depart, I will send him unto you And when he is come, he will reprove the world of sin, and of righteousness, and of judgment:
Of sin, because they believe not on me;
Of righteousness, because I go to my Father, and ye see me no more;
Of judgment, because the prince of this world is judged. .-***John 16:7-11***

## We cry to God

We spend a lot of time crying to God, asking why me? We do a lot of praying, begging God to fix the situation, but we do not use the weapons he has given us. I can imagine God is standing as a parent filled with pain for a child, who is being bullied. The child does not understand that he has everything he needs to stop the suffering, if he would only use what he has been given.

I wasted much time feeling sorry for myself. I did not go to God for the help I needed until I started going to church with my children. I had suppressed most of the memories, but the pain was still there. I was able to recall the painful experiences as I got on my knees and prayed to God. I felt secure in God's presence, so I could remember things and talk to God about them. I continued to talk to God as if he were my friend. I studied his words and I took them into my heart. Because of the abuse, I felt dirty, ashamed and worthless. Because no one I loved listened to me or protected me, I felt rejected. God's love, through his words, made me realize that those things were lies. He let me know I did not have to feel rejected, because I belong to him. The lies that had once filled me began to be replaced with the truth. The truth began to set me free!

We have to understand that the devil has no mercy. He will attack from the smallest to the largest and from the weakest to the strongest. While we are crying, the enemy is glad for our weakness. He is plotting another attack that is even greater than the last.

In this life, you may face pain that will feel as though someone is pulling the guts right out of your live, conscious body, yet it will not kill you. Please get on your knees to God and have your cry. Ask God to send people and resources into your life that will help you repair the damage. Use the mind God gave you to get help for your problem if possible.

I actually began to have therapy with God. When I prayed to God telling him about the memories I had been suppressing, that was therapy. We are hesitant to seek therapy because we believe it says we are weak. Sometimes we are weak. There is only so much a human being can handle. I decided to go to a therapist for help. I realized that I had been pushing the painful memories back in my mind, but the psychological result from them affected my living.

When my children were young boys, John took care of us all. I was not able to handle being a mother. I was not able to handle much at all. I was always depressed. My behavior was, what I consider now, unbearable. I do not think John knew how negatively, influenced I was from my past, when we first met. He never gave up on me though. I did not sleep well at night. Whenever I started to fall asleep, I became terrified. The fear I felt as a child would come, as I drifted off to sleep. I had nightmares. I did not know healthy love. I wanted to love and I did care for my family, but what I knew was abuse. John was extremely patient and understanding. He helped me to understand what love is. I believe God sent him into my life for that purpose.

During therapy, I learned that an adult with buried issues from childhood must get help from a professional. Simply going to another person will not help you to resolve all your complicated issues. You do not understand them and the other person will not understand either. Those of you who try to escape with drugs, alcohol or other abusive behavior will not escape that way. I know you exist, because I have met some of you. I have been where you are.

I am telling my story to help many who are ashamed. That is the stigma with childhood sexual abuse. Many times people do not get help, because they are afraid of what people may say. The people who are talking poorly about you will not help you anyway. Who cares what they say! Victims have to help one another. People who have unkind words to say do so foolishly, not considering themselves. God loves you the same as anyone else. We are all in this world in the same condition. We need love.

As a child, you are not able to understand many things. Since there was no one to help me process experiences nor to console me, I developed a unique way of surviving. I turned inside myself for help. I stored the disturbing experiences inside me until later, when I could understand. I learned that this is a common method of survival for some abused children. I was protecting the little girl, because the pain and disturbance were too much for her. I grew up, but a part of me was sheltered inside myself as that little girl. Through the process of therapy, I saw things as an adult that I had been remembering through the eyes of a child. I expressed the terror that I did not know was there for so many years. I discovered and expressed the crushing pain of feeling unloved, by my mother, whom I loved so much. I understood things that a little girl could not understand.

As an adult, I always felt confused and in an emotional uproar. As the little girl was relieved of her terror, the fear of falling asleep began to leave. It still aches that I do not have a normal relationship with my mother, but I understand it is not all my responsibility. My emotions are more stable. Through therapy and God's love, through his word, I have become free from much hurt and confusion.

I know it is easy to feel sorry for yourself, but you cannot be consumed with pity. Go to the word with vigor and determination and let God heal your pain, then get up and fight! "But he was wounded for our transgressions, he was bruised for our iniquities: the chastisement of our peace was upon him; and with his stripes we are healed." -*Isaiah 53:5* Don't you remember? You are on the winning side. You are not dying; you are wounded and God will heal it. Jesus already died for you. "But God commendeth his love toward us, in that, while we were yet sinners, Christ died for us."- ***Romans 5:8*** Hallelujah!

**GOD LOVES YOU!**

All scripture is given by inspiration of God, and is profitable for doctrine, for reproof, for correction, for instruction in righteousness:-*II Timothy 3:16*

## You have joined forces with God

I have two sons. The youngest is in the National Guard Reserve going to college and he served in the U. S. Army for six years. I told him one day, that I hoped he would not have to go to war. His response to me was a puzzled look, asking me the question, "Ma what do you think the army is for?" My oldest son served in the U. S. Marine Corps. When he was deployed to Afghanistan in 2002, I reacted as if I did not realize he might have to go to war. What was I thinking?

U. S. Soldiers train vigorously for nine weeks in basic training to be ready for war-*www.goarmy.com*. The men and women join knowing that they will be training for war. They understand that there will be injury and suffering. They focus on their mission. They fight with a focus on the love for their great nation. They nurse and heal the wounded and they fight on. They do not stop fighting until the battle is over and each side puts their weapons away.

These soldiers do not stop fighting because of injury or pain or death.

When we give our hearts to the Lord, I do not know what we are thinking. I do not believe we fully understand, that the profession we make signs us up for a battle. Do we understand we have joined forces with Almighty God?

As Christians, our enemy is the devil. How much more vigorously should we be prepared? How much more should we be focused on the love that we have for our Savior? How much more determined should we be to fight until the end?

## GOD LOVES YOU!

Are not two sparrows sold for a farthing? and one of them shall not fall on the ground without your Father.
But the very hairs of your head are all numbered.
Fear ye not therefore, ye are of more value than many sparrows. -*Matthew 10:29-31*

Casting all your care upon him; for he careth for you. - *I Peter 5:7*

But my God shall supply all your need according to his riches in glory by Christ Jesus. -*Philippians 4:19*

## Basic Combat Training

As a soldier in God's army, you need to get training. When you attend classes that teach the bible, you are training. The bible tells us that we must study. "Study to shew thyself approved unto God, a workman that needeth not to be ashamed, rightly dividing the word of truth." -*II Timothy 2:15*

I have been in many bible studies and many Sunday school classes. They are usually not very large groups of people. Even in churches where the number of the congregation is in the thousands, the classes are very small in comparison. Many times extremely large churches need to have at least two worship services and maybe three. This is not true for the bible studies, where there is opportunity to ask questions. Why is this? Do we go to church to socialize only? Is it that we do not realize what we forfeit, when we are not taught God's word? The bible tells us that the word is good for many things we need to be strong soldiers. "All scripture is given by inspiration of

God, and is profitable for doctrine, for reproof, for correction, for instruction in righteousness:" *-II Timothy 3:16*
I enjoy attending the classes where I can be taught God's word and I am able to ask questions.

Read the bible regularly and memorize scripture. "Thy word have I hid in mine heart, that I might not sin against thee."*-Psalm 119:11*
Our hearts should be filled with the word. Temptation is always there. Remember the word is your sword. You need to be able to exercise authority over evil immediately. You will not usually have time to get your bible out and look for scriptures.

You must be careful of the company you keep. You know that birds of a feather really do flock together, don't you? You cannot spend much time with someone who is not of God. "Blessed is the man that walketh not in the counsel of the ungodly, nor standeth in the way of sinners, nor sitteth in the seat of the scornful. But his delight is in the law of the LORD; and in his law doth he meditate day and night.   And he shall be like a tree planted by the rivers of water, that bringeth forth his fruit in his season; his leaf also shall not wither; and whatsoever he doeth shall prosper."-*Psalm 1:1-3*   I know it can be tempting to keep company with people who are not trying to live a holy life.   The fun they seem to be having can be enticing.   Walking with God sometimes feels lonely.    I try to remember that with God I am filled with joy, I am protected, I am completely loved.

Choose the things you see and the things you hear carefully. "Keep thy heart with all diligence; for out of it are the issues of life." *-Proverbs 4:23*   The things you allow into your heart make you who you are.   If it does not line up with the word of God, do not watch it, do not listen to it. Set in your mind the person you desire to be.   Watch the things that take you in that direction. Listen to the things that bring your thoughts toward that goal.

Keep a keen focus on the Lord. Pass by the gossip, confusion and other traps. I call them traps because they will catch you and have you tied up. You will forget about the complete happiness you have in Jesus. These things will make you feel unhappy, when you should be filled with the joy of the Lord. "…for the joy of the LORD is your strength." *-Nehemiah 8:10*

## JESUS LOVES YOU!

These things I have spoken unto you, that in me ye might have peace. In the world ye shall have tribulation: but be of good cheer; I have overcome the world. *-John 16:3*3

## You are a soldier; Fight!

Be watchful! be diligent! "…Be strong in the Lord and in the power of his might." *-**Ephesians 6:10***. Be well equipped with the armor God provides each one of us. When the devil has knocked you to your knees, get back up with all the rage he has stirred up in you and fight. Get up! Get angry! Fight stronger! Fight harder! Laugh in his face. Let him know that you are a soldier willing to go all the way with the Lord. Let him know that you will let nothing stop you. Say to him aloud, that no injury will hold you back. Tell him, though your knees are bloodied, your hands are blistered and your eyes are filled with tears, you will fight on!

I say these things to the devil to constantly remind him that he will not have victory in my life. I will fight for the Lord no matter what the devil attacks me with. I will always have victory; I am with the winner! "Who shall separate us from the love of Christ? shall tribulation, or distress, or persecution, or famine, or nakedness, or peril, or sword?" -***Romans 8:35***

"For I am persuaded, that neither death, nor life, nor angels, nor principalities, nor powers, nor things present, nor things to come,"

"Nor height, nor depth, nor any other creature, shall be able to separate us from the love of God, which is in Christ Jesus our Lord. " -***Romans 8:38, 39***

When I began studying and trusting in God, I was still in great pain, but the pain lessened as I got closer to God. While you are fighting, you are coming out of your situation.   You are maturing as a Christian. You are learning more and more about God. You are giving God the glory. You are the soldier he equips you to be.

You will begin to understand what your specific assignment is in the church. God has blessed you with abilities and gifts that will help you complete your assignment. "And God hath set some in the church, first apostles, secondarily prophets, thirdly Teachers, after that miracles, then gifts of healings, helps, governments, diversities of tongues."-*I Corinthians 12:28*

What do you enjoy doing? What is it that fulfills you? That is the thing God expects you to use to complete your assignment in ministry. It will not be difficult for you to recognize.

When you understand what your assignment is, do it with great tenacity. This will help you defeat the devil's evil plans. Your ministry will do what he hates. It will bring others to Christ.

## JESUS LOVES YOU!

For the Lord himself shall descend from heaven with a shout, with the voice of the archangel, and with the trump of God: and the dead in Christ shall rise first:
Then we which are alive and remain shall be caught up together with them in the clouds, to meet the Lord in the air: and so shall we ever be with the Lord. - ***I Thessalonians 4:16, 17***

In a moment, in the twinkling of an eye, at the last trump: for the trumpet shall sound, and the dead shall be raised incorruptible, and we shall be changed. - ***I Corinthians 15:52***

And behold, I am coming quickly, and My reward is with Me, to give to every one according to his work.-***Revelation 22:12***

# The Greatest Love Story Ever Told

I have felt God's love so intensely, that I have no doubt of his unconditional love for me. I have felt like God has carried me in his arms like a baby. He has nurtured me like a mother would. He has protected me like a father would. Many times in my life I did not care about myself. I did not value my life. I placed myself in dangerous situations. With God's love, through his word, I know that I am special and I should expect love. Many times God has allowed me to clearly know his love.

It continues to be painful and unfortunate, that I have never had a good relationship with my mother. I have discovered that a person must recognize his or her own needs. No matter how much you want help for them, they have to want it and accept it themselves. While I continue to pray for that situation, God cares for me as a parent would. Whenever I am going the wrong way, the Lord gently stops me and redirects my path.

I was alone with my sons during a very trying time. They were both teenagers, and they began to behave like some young men do without a male guardian. Sometimes I thought I did not even know who they were. I could no longer get them to church. They were not going to school the way they should have. I thought the people they were spending time with were scary. I was afraid to leave my house, because I was worried about what would be going on, when I was gone. I began to be afraid for their lives. I started drinking, so I could go to sleep at night.

When I noticed the road I was going down, I began to pray harder and more often, seeking God's face. Once while I was praying I heard a voice say, "I have always taken care of your sons and I will continue to take care of them." As I prayed I saw a vision of my sons, with a bright light shining down on them. I believed it was the voice of God comforting me. I believed that, because I knew I had not known how to care for my children. It was evident to me that

God had been caring for them. I was becoming physically ill and would not have rest thinking my children were in danger. I believe God, like a loving parent wanted to end my fears. The comfort of knowing your children will be taken care of by the Lord is beyond any words.

My children have gone through much in the last 11 years, but God has been with them. Many times I have needed wisdom to help guide them and God has always been there, through his word, to lead the way. They have been law-abiding citizens, husbands and parents.

My oldest son went to Afghanistan after the 9-11 attack on the United States. I was greatly fearful for him, but I prayed. After prayer I realized, that the only life worth living is a life lived for God, unto a death going to heaven to be with God. I knew he was saved, so he would go to heaven if his life was not spared. I had peace, while he was in Afghanistan. My son returned home safely. My youngest son served in the U. S. Army from 2003 to 2009, during this time of war, remaining unharmed the entire time. I continue to have rest knowing the Lord is in control.

In 2005, a hurricane named Katrina devastated New Orleans, Louisiana. I was there at that time, but I was unharmed during the storm. As a result of the storm, I had no employment and nowhere to live. I decided to move to Atlanta, Georgia.

While in Atlanta, I began to feel disoriented. I was in the hospital one day, during a general visit, looking at the identification band placed on my arm. It had my age on it. I laughed to myself because I thought the age was wrong. After a few minutes, I realized that the age had to be right according to my birth date. I had somehow lost a year of time in my mind. I decided I needed to seek help.

I realized during counseling, that I was nearing a breakdown. The process of abruptly losing a whole existence and trying to start another one, proved to be too much for me. I believe God kept me and would not let me break. The counselors could not understand why I was doing so well, after hearing my entire story. They did not understand why I was a normal, functioning adult. I understood that it had been God. This time it was also God, my father, snatching me from destruction. I give God the glory and I thank him for showing me his love.

At last, the abused, rejected little girl that survived inside me is gone now. She was here for a long time, looking for someone to heal her and understand her deep pain. The emotionally, psychologically troubled woman she became is also gone. God saved them by his blood. God has raised them and empowered them through his word. God comforted and consoled them through his grace, mercy and kindness. If you see me and you try to find either one of them, you will not. Your search would be in vain, because they are gone. "Therefore if any man be in Christ, he is a new creature: old things are passed away; behold, all things are become new."-*II Corinthians 5:17*

I finally realize, no matter the trials that come my way I must always turn to God. Turning away from God is irrational for me now. The other option would be to turn towards the enemy, the devil. God is the lover of my soul. I depend on the Lord, through his word, to validate me and not man. God created me, so he knows me and he has a plan for my life. When I am with God, I am a soldier on the winning side.

**God Loves You!**
God loves you with the depth and intensity that no one will ever love you. He knows you are special just the way you are and he will encourage and nurture you, so you may become all he created you to be. He understands and accepts your frailties. He has mercy on you and patience with you. He gave the life of his only son for you.

Jesus loves you. He gave his life freely so that you might live eternally. He left heaven to come down to earth and show you how to live a life pleasing to God. He died in your place so that you would not face eternal damnation. He died and paid the price for the sins you committed. It was the price you could never have paid. He had great compassion for your great weakness.

He went to heaven to sit at the right hand of the father, but he would not leave you alone in this evil world. He sent the Comforter to guide you down the right path of life. He sent the precious Holy Spirit.

God wants you to feel his loving embrace everyday. He wants your thoughts and desires to be pure. He wants you to walk in the pathway of right living. He inspired men to write down the words that hold the wisdom you need to defeat the enemy in this wicked world. This is God's wisdom, which is valuable for reprimand, principle teaching and instruction in righteousness.

In a moment that we do not know, Jesus will come back to get you. He loves you and would not leave you in this wicked world. He is coming back to take you to heaven to be with him forever. He will give you a new body not fallible like the old one. He will reward you according to the work you have done. Nothing you do for the Lord will be in vain.

Are you able to see now, how everything God does is for YOU? YOU are the object of his affection. YOU are the one he loves. YOU put a twinkle in his eye and a smile on his face. He loves YOU so tenderly that he knows how many hairs are on your head. He loves every detail concerning YOU. You can go to him with any problem or concern you have. He always has time for YOU. He does not want you to be without what you need. He will give you all you need, because he has everything. His desire is to give it all to YOU.

I am talking about the kind of love that drives away fear. This kind of love calms and gives peace during the extremely painful times. It is the love you will never find anywhere else, though you may look high and low. I do not simply mean a love I have heard of many times. I do not simply mean a love I have read of many times. I am writing of a love that I feel from day to day. I am writing of a love having all the compassion, mercy, kindness and strength you need to fight like a fully equipped soldier in God's army.

Would you agree with me? Have you ever known a love greater than the love God has for mankind? He loves you so, that he has had me to live this life and witness to you about his love for me. If he does it for me, he will do it for you. "For there is no respect of persons with God." -***Romans 2:11***
Now with truth, righteousness, the gospel of peace, faith, salvation, the word of God, prayer and this great love, Fight on soldiers! Fight on! Amen.

Made in the USA
Charleston, SC
08 July 2010